The Tax Reform Act of 2014 makes the code simpler and fairer by:

- Providing a significantly more generous standard deduction so that 95 percent of taxpayers will no longer be forced to itemize their individual tax deductions.

- Reducing the size of the federal income tax code by 25 percent.

- Tackling fraud, abuse and mismanagement at the IRS to protect hard-earned taxpayer dollars.

It will make our economy stronger resulting in:

- $3.4 trillion in additional economic growth.

- 1.8 million new jobs.

- $1,300 per year more in the pockets of middle-class American families.

The results are clear:

✓ **More Growth.**

✓ **More Jobs.**

✓ **More money in the pockets of middle-class families.**

On October 22, 1986, President Ronald Reagan signed into law the Tax Reform Act of 1986, a bill that would become known as the single largest simplification of the U.S. tax code in history. President Reagan's signature on that landmark legislation marked the end of a federal tax code that was too costly, too complex and too confusing — and which totaled over 26,300 pages. It set into motion a transformation that would lower tax rates for families and job creators to worldwide lows and, by 1990, would save the American middle class family of four more than $9,000 in taxes that they would have owed just a decade earlier.

That was nearly 30 years ago. And, despite those great accomplishments, time and meddling by politicians in Washington have taken a toll. **Today's tax code is once again a broken mess. The 26,000-page tax code of 1986 has grown to more than 70,000 pages. In the last decade alone, there have been more than 4,400 changes to the code — more than one a day.** And America, once the beacon for investment, hiring and strong wages, is now falling behind our foreign competitors as our corporate tax rate stands as the highest in the developed world.

A European government official once referred to America's strong economic policies as "the American miracle." Today, though, our broken tax code is a contributing factor to many of the economic challenges we are facing — stubbornly high unemployment, stagnant wages and a seemingly increasing inability to achieve the American Dream.

America can, and must, do better. Our plan, the Tax Reform Act of 2014, addresses these problems by fixing our broken tax code so that it works for American families and job creators by:

- **Making the tax code simpler and fairer for families and employers.**
- **Strengthening the economy by lowering tax rates so there are more jobs and bigger paychecks for hardworking taxpayers.**

For instance, estimates from the non-partisan Joint Committee on Taxation and calculations based on their data show — without increasing the budget deficit — the Tax Reform Act of 2014 could:

- **Allow roughly 95 percent of filers to get the lowest possible tax rate by simply claiming the standard deduction (no more need to itemize and track receipts).**
- **Increase take-home pay for a family of four earning $51,000 (median U.S. income) by $1,300.**
- **Create up to 1.8 million new private sector jobs.**

The legislation would accomplish these goals, in part, **by reducing the size of the federal income tax code by 25 percent.**

DEFINING THE PROBLEM

Today's Tax Code is Too Complex, Too Costly and Too Unfair

Problem: The Complexity of the Tax Code Makes It Unfair to Hardworking Taxpayers

Every year, families and businesses find themselves in the midst of tax season trudging through last year's receipts attempting to compile all the necessary documentation required to file their taxes. The tax code is so complex that nearly three-quarters of Americans feel like they have no idea what they are doing when they file their taxes. For those who pay a professional to do their taxes, it still feels like a leap of faith — having no real way of knowing if the preparer got it right. Driving this fear and unease is the fact that a simple mistake could mean a fine, or worse, an audit.

Let's face it: the IRS tax code is a nightmare. It is too complex, too costly and too unfair. As taxpayers struggle to comply with our tax laws, they feel as though Washington is working against them. They wonder whether the neighbor down the street, who can afford some high-priced lawyer or accountant, got a better deal.

Given that frustration and lack of fairness, it comes as little surprise that when asked, **over 80 percent of Americans agree that:**

- The complexity of **the tax code benefits corporations and special interests** who can afford lawyers and accountants at the expense of average taxpayers.
- The complexity of our **tax code hurts the economy.**
- **They are angrier about how Washington spends their money** than about the amount of money they pay in taxes.

Today's tax code is more than 70,000 pages and requires the average taxpayer to spend about 13 hours gathering all the receipts, reading all the rules and filling out all the forms the IRS requires to file their taxes. In her 2013 annual report to Congress, the National Taxpayer Advocate, Nina E. Olson, identified the complexity of the tax code as, "the #1 most serious problem facing taxpayers." She recommended that Congress take steps to overhaul a code that "obscures comprehension."

Given that reality, it is no wonder that over **90 percent of us either pay someone else to do our taxes, or purchase commercial software** to help us do it ourselves. All totaled, **Americans spend over $160 billion and about 6 billion hours a year trying to comply with the tax code.**

Roughly two-thirds of Americans know that the reason the code is so complex is the bewildering array of credits, deductions, rules and regulations. For example, families struggling to afford quality education for their children have to wade through **15 different education tax breaks.** To find out whether they qualify for any of them, they have to go through **90 pages of IRS instructions.** It is enough to make anyone want to pull their hair out.

When it comes to the tax code there is widespread agreement that everyone should play by the same rules. An individual's tax rate should be determined by what's fair, not who they know in Washington.

Unfortunately, the tax code has been riddled with lobbyist loopholes that pick winners and losers based on what favors Washington was handing out. It is no wonder that so many Americans are frustrated. **Simplifying the broken tax code by eliminating lobbyist loopholes and treating hardworking taxpayers fairly is why we need tax reform.**

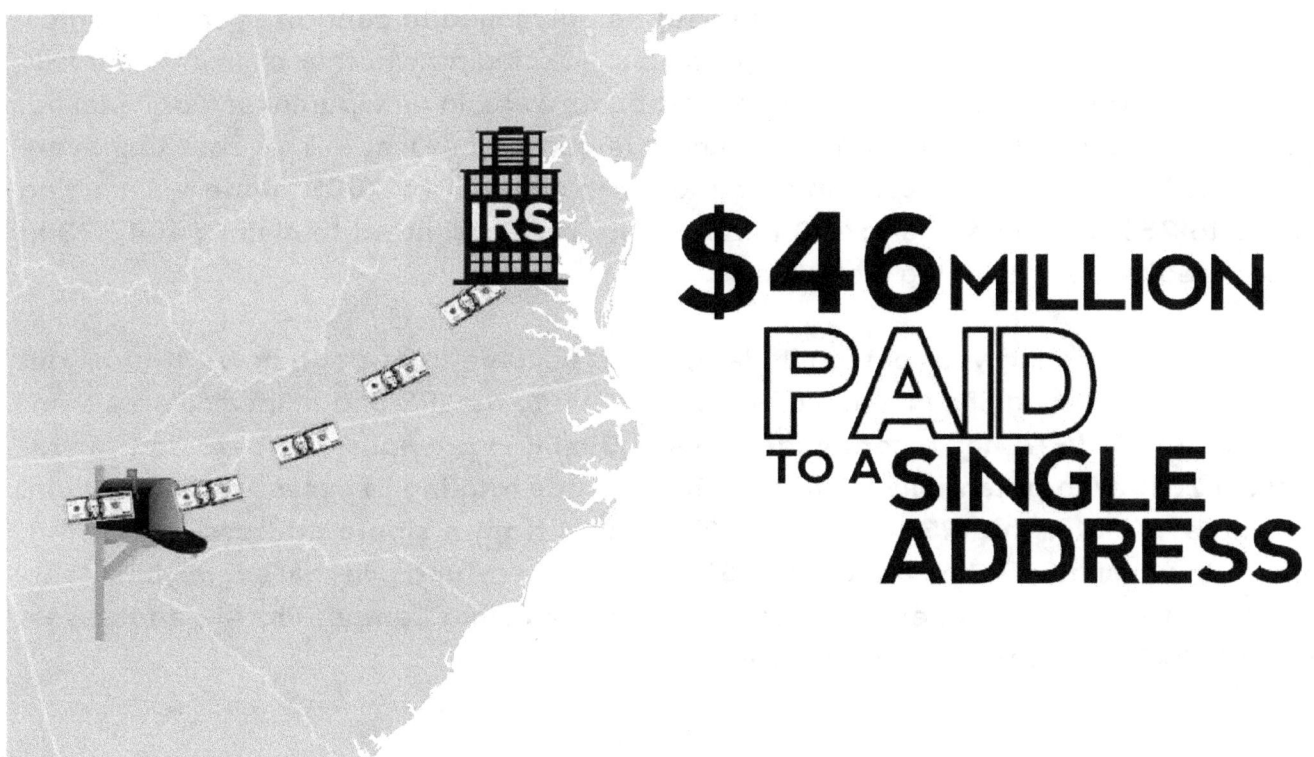

Problem: The Complexity of the Tax Code Allows Washington to Waste Your Tax Dollars

Not only is the way Washington takes your money unfair, it wastes the money it takes from you. **In one case, the IRS sent nearly 24,000 refunds totaling over $46 million to a single address.** It doesn't end there. The IRS has a long history of mismanaging hard-earned taxpayer dollars.

This is particularly true of existing refundable tax credit programs, where the IRS is unwilling or unable to stop the waste, fraud and abuse. For example, **over the last 10 years, the IRS erroneously sent out an estimated $132 billion of your tax dollars to false claimants.** The Earned Income Tax Credit (EITC), the largest refundable tax credit, consistently ranks among the worst government programs in terms of waste, fraud and abuse — even though it is one of the most important tools to help low-income, working Americans. Last year, 21 to 25 percent of all EITC payments were incorrect, costing American taxpayers as much as $13.6 billion.

There are other sources of waste, too. For example, the Additional Child Tax Credit (ACTC), despite being based on wages earned, only requires that a claimant provide an Individual Taxpayer Identification Number (ITIN). Unlike a Social Security Number (SSN), an ITIN is available to non-citizens who are not authorized to work in the United States. According to the Treasury Inspector General for Tax Administration (TIGTA), **between 2000 and 2010, ACTC claims by individuals not authorized to work in the United States rose from $62 million per year to roughly $4.2 billion per year,** despite the fact that such individuals cannot legally earn the income that is necessary to qualify for the credit.

These are only a few examples. Energy-related tax credits also are rife with waste and mismanagement. TIGTA reports that the IRS has repeatedly failed to confirm even basic information for those claiming residential energy credits — including whether claimants actually owned a home; whether energy improvement products were, in fact, purchased or installed; or even the address of the home on which improvements were made. This **cost taxpayers at least $234 million in wasteful and fraudulent payments in 2009 alone** — including payments to **262 prisoners and to 100 minors who were permitted to claim $404,578 in improper credits,** despite being ineligible.

In an era where securing your personal identity has become front page news, it turns out that identity theft is a significant source of lost revenue to the IRS and of incalculable damage to taxpayers. **TIGTA has recently identified 1.5 million previously undetected tax returns from 2010 with potentially fraudulent tax refunds totaling in excess of $5.2 billion.** For example, in 2010, **the IRS received 2,137 returns from a single address in Lansing, Michigan, to which the IRS paid a total of $3.3 million in refunds.** In that same year, **nearly 89,000 potentially fraudulent returns were received from Tampa, Florida addresses, resulting in $468 million in improper payments.**

Problem: An Agency Out of Control

It is widely acknowledged that there is one government agency the American people fear more than any other (and with good reason) – the IRS. **An IRS audit can tangle a taxpayer in a nightmare of paperwork and legal fees.** If that were not bad enough, over the last year we have learned how the IRS targeted individuals based on their personal beliefs.

The IRS became the subject of intense public scrutiny in May 2013, when it was revealed that agency officials used inappropriate criteria in selecting 501(c)(4) tax-exempt applications for audits and reviews based on their political beliefs.

Though the investigation is not complete, and the Obama Administration has yet to turn over documentation critical to fully and thoroughly investigating the actions of the agency, we do know that the IRS leaked confidential taxpayer information, delayed applications of groups supporting conservative causes and threatened conservatives with higher taxes. Furthermore, on November 29, 2013, the Obama Administration issued new proposed regulations on 501(c)(4) organizations, the first rule change in more than 50 years, to restrict their First Amendment rights.

Because of the complexity in the tax code, the IRS cannot safeguard hard-earned taxpayer dollars, but it can use that same complexity to target ordinary Americans based on their political beliefs. Reforming the tax code is the only way to rein in an agency that is clearly out of control.

Problem: The Complexity in the Tax Code is Stifling Investment, Hiring and Wages

In late 2013, as the Dow Jones Industrial Average hit an all-time high of 16,000, many on Wall Street marked the milestone. For everyday Americans, though, the stock market is not the measurement they use to determine how they are doing. For them, it boils down to simpler measures – whether they have a job, whether they have received a raise, the amount of money in their checking account, and if they have saved enough for their children's college or their own retirement.

While the stock market may be up, paychecks for ordinary Americans are flat or down. That is why **more than 68 percent of Americans think the country is in the same place or worse off than in 2009,** when the President first took office. According to a NBC/Wall Street Journal poll, **it has been a decade since even 40 percent of Americans thought we were headed in the right direction.**

While the unemployment rate has started to drift downward, too much of that decline is because Americans have simply given up even looking for work. **In December 2012 alone, for instance, more than half a million people simply dropped out of the labor force. Not in 36 years – since the Carter Administration – has the labor force participation rate been so low.** If those individuals were added back into the calculation, America would have an **unemployment rate of more than 11 percent.**

A **WEAK** ECONOMY

Americans dropping out of the workforce

College graduates unemployed or underemployed

Smaller middle class paychecks

What job growth we have seen isn't nearly enough. The lack of jobs is especially being felt by college graduates. Our economy is so weak that it cannot take care of the kids graduating from college, as **52 percent of recent college graduates are either unemployed or underemployed.**

Those Americans who have been able to hold onto their job during the worst economic recovery in history have sacrificed bigger paychecks for it. **Middle class incomes have fallen over the last four years by more than 5 percent.** At the same time, prices for items like home heating oil, groceries and health care have steadily risen.

What is the President's answer to the lack of good jobs in America? According to his budgets, it is adding even more complexity to the tax code, more tax increases and even more debt. The President's budget never balances, and his refusal to deal with Washington spending leads to skyrocketing debt and deficits. This only makes our economic problems worse. During the President's own Commission on Fiscal Responsibility, economist Dr. Carmen Reinhart testified that once a nation's total debt equaled 90 percent of its gross domestic product, that debt becomes a drag on economic growth. In fact, it would slow growth by about one percent a year. That translates into about 1 million jobs in the United States.

The problem in Washington isn't too little revenue, it is too much wasteful spending. Although the Budget Control Act and the December 2013 budget agreement included modest steps to reduce spending, these reforms are not enough. While Congress continues to work to address the long-term budget situation, an immediate challenge facing job creators of all sizes is the broken tax code.

Our broken tax code is like a wet blanket on the economy — smothering the job creation and wage increases Americans need. In addition to maddening complexity, **small businesses face tax rates as high as 44.6 percent, U.S. corporations face the highest combined Federal-State corporate tax rate in the industrialized world at 39.1 percent, and the United States has an outdated international tax system designed nearly 50 years ago when we faced virtually no foreign competition.**

Because of the tax code, America is losing ground. **In 1960, U.S.-headquartered companies comprised 17 of the world's 20 largest companies. By 2010, just six of the top 20 companies were headquartered in the United States.** At the same time, our foreign competitors are actively reforming their tax laws and we are falling even further behind. The tax code is so outdated and uncompetitive that it makes the United States a less attractive place to invest and hire.

Our outdated international tax system actually encourages American businesses to keep profits and jobs outside of America. A recent analysis of news stories highlighted **more than 25 public companies that have either relocated or considered relocation of U.S.–based operations overseas since 1998.** Taxes were an oft-cited reason throughout the report. News reports detailed well-known companies that have either reincorporated in other countries or have moved operations, including jobs, overseas and have lowered their tax burden in the process. Companies that have made business changes resulting in lower tax rates include Cisco which, in 2011, according to news reports, moved eight different companies to Ireland where the corporate tax rate is 12.5 percent. Not far behind was Eaton Corporation, which in 2012, bought Cooper Industries, PLC and moved its headquarters from Cleveland to Ireland. According to *Bloomberg News,* the company expected to save $160 million in tax costs from the move.

A 2008 *Reuters* news report noted that,
"Foreign ownership of U.S. companies more than doubled from 1996 to 2005 measured by revenue and more than tripled as measured by assets, according to an analysis of U.S. tax data."

America's high tax rates also make U.S.-based companies attractive targets for foreign ownership. Perhaps one of the best-known examples is Anheuser-Busch, which was bought by Belgian brewer InBev in 2008. As *Bloomberg* wrote at the time of the announcement, "The deal would be the second largest takeover of a U.S. consumer goods company...." It is clear that America's tax code, both its outdated international tax rules and its prohibitively high corporate rate, are making American companies less competitive against their foreign rivals. In testimony before Congress, James Zrust of Boeing described the acute challenges presented at home and abroad by the high corporate tax rate in the United States, stating:

"*Although a significant portion of our customers are outside of the United States, our employees, manufacturing and support operations, research and development activities and intellectual property are predominantly located in the United States. Historically, over 95 percent of our net income is attributable to these domestic activities. In addition to a significant percentage of our customers being outside of the U.S., many of our competitors are as well. It is well known that our largest commercial competitor is located in Europe, and new competition is rapidly emerging from China, Canada, Brazil, and Russia-all with lower combined federal and local statutory tax rates than the United States... We can no longer deny that capital is mobile... Recently, a commercial aircraft customer located in the Middle East approached Boeing with a concern regarding the lack of U.S. companies willing to bid on a contract in that region. The general sentiment is that price bids received from companies based in Asia, Europe and Australia are consistently lower than those made by U.S. aerospace companies due to our tax system and high corporate rate."*

Boeing has more than 160,000 employees in 34 states, but the challenge imposed by the corporate rate is not limited to corporate employers of that size.

Neenah Foundry in Neenah, Wisconsin is a 141-year old manufacturer producing materials for both industrial and commercial purposes and is a leading supplier of municipal castings including manhole frames, lids and grates, trench castings and decorative tree grates as well as other materials. With more than 2,100 employees, and seven plants across the United States, they may not be as large as some other well-known corporations, but they are greatly impacted by the high U.S. corporate rate.

Discussing how the high corporate rate affects planning and investment decisions, Tom Riordan of Neenah Foundry noted that, **"The high corporate rate impacts cash flow and restricts growth, making it difficult to predict future business expansion plans."** Riordan added that if the corporate rate were lower, **"The savings could be used to improve processes and make tooling upgrades, both of which help support continued growth of our business and the local economy."**

Simply put, if taxes were not so high and tax compliance costs so prohibitive, businesses would have the resources to reinvest in their businesses and help grow the economy of their communities.

Our broken tax code does not affect only corporate job creators. According to the non-partisan Joint Committee on Taxation, small businesses generate roughly half of total business income earned in the United States. These small businesses and pass-through entities are especially sensitive to tax rates and the complexity of the tax code. Research by the National Federation of Independent Business (NFIB) finds that **75 percent of small businesses are unincorporated pass-through entities, so owners report business income on their personal tax returns.** Yet, those same business owners face high tax compliance costs that inhibit investment, growth and hiring.

9 out of 10 small business owners rely on an outside tax preparer

Lacking tax expertise, nearly nine out of every ten small business owners rely on an outside tax preparer. That comes at a cost. **Tax compliance costs are 65 percent higher for small businesses than for big businesses. Compliance costs small-business owners $18-$19 billion per year. Paperwork costs come to $74.24 per hour.**

Small business owners benefit greatly from the certainty of lower rates and permanency in the code.

In testimony before Congress, Sam Griffith, President and CEO, National Jet Company, Inc., Cumberland, Maryland said, **"Most Members of Congress probably only think about the AMT in terms of its impact on the average 'middle class' family."**

Griffith's testimony highlighted other limitations that AMT places on his business making it harder to plan and invest. His testimony concluded with a comment on the lack of certainty created by the code stating, "We can't just purchase a machine on December 31st by midnight based on a vote Congress just took. It takes time to place this equipment in service even if we had the free capital to make a last minute multi-million dollar purchase based on Congressional action, or inaction."

With **about half of the private sector workforce employed by small businesses – a total of nearly 60 million Americans – tax rates as high as 44.6 percent** and compliance costs resulting from a broken tax code impose economic pressure on small businesses, weaken our economy, hurt job creation and reduce take home pay for workers. Every dollar small businesses spend on taxes and tax compliance is a dollar they do not have to invest in equipment, start a new production line, hire a new employee or provide more in wages and benefits.

Closing Loopholes to Spend More Is Really Just a Tax Increase – Not a Solution

Some in Washington believe that when a loophole is closed, that money should go for new spending instead of lower taxes. Tax reform should not be an excuse for the government to take more out of the economy and pockets of taxpayers to fund more Washington bailouts. Instead, tax reform should simplify the code and lower rates so businesses of all sizes can create new jobs and increase workers' take-home pay.

Americans deserve a simpler, fairer tax code that leads to more jobs, more take home pay and better benefits for their families.

Fixing our broken tax code is the right thing to do, but we need to act. Because the longer we wait, the further America will fall behind. Fewer jobs will be created, take-home pay will remain stagnant, and families will continue to struggle. **America can't afford to wait. Now is the time for Congress to fix our broken tax code.**

THE PLAN

Understanding the problem, we can now craft the solution. Fixing our broken tax code will accomplish two critical goals:

1. **MAKE THE TAX CODE SIMPLER AND FAIRER FOR FAMILIES AND EMPLOYERS.**

2. **STRENGTHEN THE ECONOMY SO THERE ARE MORE JOBS AND BIGGER PAY-CHECKS FOR AMERICAN FAMILIES.**

These goals are not mutually exclusive, and looking back to 1986, they can both be achieved through a single piece of legislation. Nearly 30 years later, the Tax Reform Act of 2014 once again achieves those two important goals.

We can have a simpler, fairer and flatter code that is more efficient and effective and that results in greater growth, more jobs and higher wages. Based on analysis by the independent, non-partisan Joint Committee on Taxation and calculations based on its data, the stronger economic growth from cleaning out the code and lowering rates means:

 $3.4 trillion in additional economic growth,

 1.8 million new jobs, and

 $1,300 per year more for the average American family.

WHAT IF WE FIXED THE TAX CODE?

The plan to fix our broken tax code is a three-step plan.

step 1 ▸ First, we make the tax code simpler and fairer, so families can do their own taxes and not wonder if someone else is getting a better deal than they are.

step 2 ▸ Second, we make the code more efficient by getting rid of special interest handouts and lowering tax rates across the board.

step 3 ▸ Third, we fix the tax code by making it more accountable to you, the taxpayer.

The results are clear:

MORE GROWTH. MORE JOBS.
MORE MONEY IN THE POCKETS OF MIDDLE-CLASS FAMILIES.

Make the Tax Code Simpler and Fairer so Families Can Do Their Own Taxes and not Wonder if Someone is Getting a Better Deal than They Are

During the Reagan Administration, the Treasury Department wrote, "A tax that places significantly different burdens on taxpayers in similar economic circumstances is not fair. For example, if two similar families have the same income, they should ordinarily pay roughly the same amount of income tax, regardless of the sources or uses of that income."

Simply put, an individual's tax bill should be determined by the taxes they owe, not who they know. That is why our plan aims to make the code simpler and fairer — so they don't have to worry whether they got a better deal than their neighbor. The extra added benefit — saving time and money on tax compliance.

Our tax reform plan reforms and simplifies a number of tax rules affecting individuals, families and job creators of all sizes.

Cut 25 percent of the Federal Income Tax - Lower Rates, Increase the Standard Deduction and Reduce the Number of Itemizers

Our plan starts off by **ripping out 25 percent of the income tax code** by eliminating lobbyist loopholes and special interest carve outs to lower rates and make the code simpler and fairer for everyone. **Today's tax code has seven rates, with a top rate of 39.6 percent.** At the end of 2012, 12 years of tax relief expired, costing American families nearly $700 billion in new taxes.

These Americans — and many small businesses — face federal tax rates as high as 44.6 percent, due in part to all the new taxes in the healthcare law. No matter how much money you make, Washington should not take nearly half of what an individual earns in federal taxes, especially not on top of all the other state and local taxes they pay.

The Tax Reform Act of 2014 reduces and collapses today's brackets into two brackets of 10 percent and 25 percent for virtually all taxable income, ensuring that over 99 percent of all taxpayers face maximum rates of 25 percent or less. That adds up. These lower rates, combined with a larger standard deduction and rising wages resulting from the legislation, will put **$1,300 more in the pockets of middle class American families.** That is money for them to help offset the ever-increasing price of groceries, gas and health care.

Current Law	Tax Reform Act of 2014
10%	10%
15%	
25%	25%
28%	
33%	
35%	
39.6%	• 25% (production income) • 35% (other income)

Right now, more than a third of all Americans are forced to itemize their deductions to ensure they pay the lowest possible tax bill. Under our plan, tax reform would make the code simpler and fairer by providing a significantly **more generous standard deduction of $11,000 for individuals and $22,000 for married couples,** which would result in far fewer taxpayers being forced to itemize their individual tax deductions, a critical component of a simpler tax code.

The non-partisan, independent Joint Committee on Taxation estimates that, under the Tax Reform Act of 2014, **nearly 95 percent of taxpayers will no longer have to itemize to ensure they aren't paying more in taxes than they owe.** Instead, they will take the newly increased standard deduction, making tax filing and compliance easier and simpler than it is today.

For families, our plan collapses six different family tax benefits (basic standard deduction, additional standard deduction, personal exemptions for taxpayer and spouse, personal exemptions for dependents, child tax credits, and head of household filing status) into three simple family tax benefits: a larger standard deduction, an additional deduction for single parents, and **an expanded child and dependent tax credit of $1,500 per child and $500 per dependent.**

In addition to these new and more generous tax benefits, the plan makes specific changes for those low-income working families who claim the highly complex Earned Income Tax Credit (EITC). The current EITC, which requires most beneficiaries to hire a tax return preparer just to claim the credit, would be simplified by converting it into an exemption of a certain amount of payroll taxes (both the employee and employer shares), which are reported directly on a worker's W-2. Depending on household circumstances, families could be shielded from as much as $4,000 in payroll tax liability. This **simplification both would eliminate the estimated $133 billion over 10 years in erroneous and fraudulent EITC payments,** and would make it easier for the roughly 25 percent of eligible families who fail to claim the EITC due to its complexity to get the tax relief they desperately need.

Helping Families Afford a Higher Education

Today's tax code contains 15 different tax breaks for higher education. Those include nine tax breaks for current expenses, two for past expenses, and four for future expenses. The IRS even has its own publication on "Tax Benefits for Education" to "help" parents figure out what they might or might not be able to access, but it is almost 90 pages long. That isn't a tax code designed for working families; it is a tax code designed to make money for accountants and tax planners.

The Tax Reform Act of 2014 simplifies the tax code and makes it easier to afford the cost of a higher education. The plan also provides greater simplicity to families by streamlining a variety of similar provisions so that they are easier to access and understand as families plan for education expenses.

Specifically, the education-related portion of **the tax reform package consolidates 15 separate education provisions into five:**

- ☑ permanent American Opportunity Tax Credit (AOTC)
- ☑ deduction for work-related education expenses
- ☑ exclusion of scholarships and grants
- ☑ gift tax exclusion for tuition payments
- ☑ tax-free 529 savings plans

Consolidating four existing tax benefits into a simplified and more valuable AOTC is based on bipartisan legislation introduced by Reps. Diane Black (R-TN) and Danny Davis (D-IL).

Their plan replaces the Hope credit, lifetime learning credit, tuition deduction, and temporary AOTC with a reformed, permanent AOTC.

Encouraging Saving for Retirement

Too often today, families struggle to save enough for retirement. According to the National Institute on Retirement Security, **for people 10 years away from retirement, the median savings is $12,000, while one-third of those between ages 55 and 64 have no retirement savings.**

Americans struggling to save for retirement face a bewildering maze of tax-preferred savings vehicles, all with their own separate, convoluted rules governing eligibility, contributions, withdrawals and other features. Our plan would make it easier to plan and save for retirement by simplifying and modernizing several existing retirement savings vehicles, while at the same time recognizing that everyone has different savings needs.

By strengthening the economy and putting an estimated $1,300 more a year in the pocket of middle-class families, Americans will have more money to save for retirement.

Our plan would not change how the tax code treats the money Americans have already saved. Going forward, it would maintain the current (2014) contribution limits for Individual Retirement Accounts (IRAs) and for defined contribution plans, like 401(k)s.

Today, when saving for retirement, a taxpayer decides whether to put the money away for retirement after taxes and save tax-free ("Roth" accounts), or put the money away tax-free and then pay taxes when they withdraw the funds during retirement ("traditional" accounts). For future contributions, our plan allows up to $8,750 (half of the contribution limit) to be contributed either to a traditional or Roth account. Any contributions in excess of $8,750 would be dedicated to a Roth-style account – making these savings tax-free during retirement. Ninety-five percent of all workers and almost 85 percent of plan participants contribute less than $8,750 per year to their retirement and therefore would be unaffected by this change.

Maintaining the American Dream of Home Ownership

Homeownership is an integral part of the American dream, and the tax code has long provided a variety of incentives to make it easier for families to buy and own a home. For many, it is the largest investment a family will ever make and serves as the cornerstone of their financial foundation.

It is important to remember that for American families, the biggest barrier to home ownership isn't a lack of tax breaks; rather, it is the lack of a job that pays enough for them to be able to buy a home. Our tax reform plan will create more jobs and put more money in the pockets of hardworking Americans – giving them more means to buy a home. In addition, our plan keeps in place tax provisions that allow ordinary Americans to own a home while trimming back provisions used only by the wealthy.

- The plan makes no changes whatsoever to the mortgage interest deduction for any current mortgage – **if you have a mortgage today, your mortgage interest deduction is unchanged.**

- The plan has no impact on future refinancing of existing mortgages.

- Current law caps the amount of mortgage interest that can be deducted at the amount associated with the first $1 million of mortgage debt. Beginning in 2015, for those taking out new mortgages, the plan would gradually and responsibly reduce the existing $1 million dollar cap so that for mortgages taken out in 2018 or later, the cap would be $500,000. This means homeowners will still be able to deduct interest on the first $500,000 of mortgage debt. (For instance, if someone buys a home for $750,000 and takes out a $600,000 mortgage, they would still be able to deduct five-sixths of their interest.) **This new cap is estimated to impact less than 5 percent of the most expensive homes on the market today.**

Simply put, **the tax reform plan completely protects *all* existing mortgages and 95 percent of all future mortgages.** These reforms and the stronger economic growth that will come with fixing our broken tax code are projected to **increase the rate of growth in home values by up to 40 percent.**

Increasing Charitable Giving – Understanding the Charitable Deduction

Charitable organizations depend upon the goodwill of the American people – the most giving and charitable people in the world.

Independent research confirms that charitable giving is closely tied to the health of the economy. Recognizing this, the Tax Reform Act of 2014 safeguards and further encourages charitable giving in several important ways, resulting in an estimated **increase in charitable giving of $2.2 billion per year.**

Because **95 percent of Americans will no longer have to itemize their taxes,** these taxpayers will no longer need to keep all the receipts and fill out all the forms necessary to claim itemized deductions like the charitable deduction – meaning they will have all the benefits of lower taxes, without all the complexity.

For the remaining five percent of Americans who under the plan choose to continue to itemize, the plan preserves the charitable deduction for contributions exceeding 2 percent of income. So, if a filer earns $100,000 and makes total contributions of $10,000, then the taxpayer would still be allowed to deduct $8,000.

Unlike other proposals over the last few years, including in the President's budget proposals, our plan does not impose any harmful cap on the amount of those charitable deductions.

Finally, the Tax Reform Act of 2014 extends the deadline for making tax deductible donations for a given tax year to April 15 of the following year (instead of December 31 of that tax year) so that individuals and families can better plan and maximize their giving.

Making the Tax Code Work Better for America's Economic Engine – Job-Creating Small Businesses

Small businesses are the driving force for economic growth and job creation in the American economy and, according to the Small Business Administration, have generated nearly two-thirds of net new jobs over recent years. Since nearly half of the private sector workforce is employed by small businesses – a total of nearly 60 million Americans – we must make sure the tax code works better for these Main Street job creators. The Tax Reform Act of 2014 accomplishes that goal by lowering rates, increasing certainty for business planning and reducing complexity. Specifically, the plan:

- Lowers tax rates across the board for small business owners who report their business income on their personal taxes and pay at individual rates, ensuring that virtually every **small business pays no more than a top rate of 25 percent.**

- Lowers the double taxation of investment income to historic lows.

- Repeals the Alternative Minimum Tax (AMT).

- Simplifies compliance through various reforms of business deductions and credits. Makes permanent section 179 expensing on as much as $250,000 in capital investments each year, including real property.

- Expands the use of "cash accounting" for businesses with gross receipts of up to $10 million, while permitting farms of all sizes to use cash accounting.

- Creates a simple, consolidated deduction for small businesses' start-up and organizational expenses.

- Simplifies the rules governing S corporations.

- Maintains current law on the estate tax, ensuring that family businesses can continue to be passed on to future generations.

The relief provided by reducing tax rates will provide greater incentives for investment and hiring and better wages. The Tax Reform Act of 2014 also provides the certainty that no business – whether a small business or a large corporation – engaged in domestic manufacturing, production, farming, extraction, or construction would be taxed at a rate higher than 25 percent. It is clear that this tax plan is all about making sure that Main Street is, and remains, "open for business."

Finally, for the roughly three percent of small businesses nationwide that are the most profitable, those businesses would also see tax relief. Their top rate will fall by almost six percentage points.

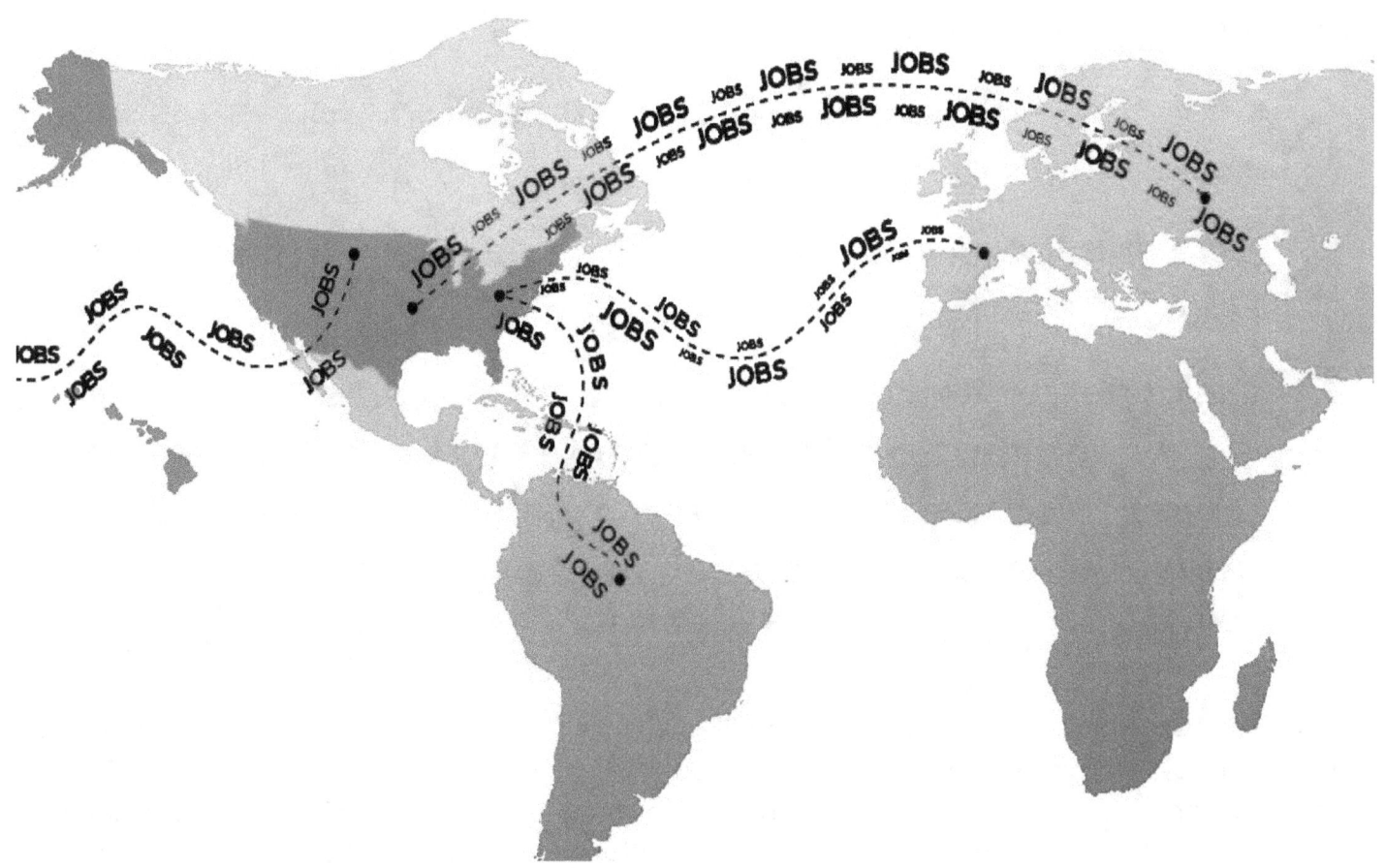

America's Larger Job Creators Win, Too

With a **reduction in the corporate rate to 25 percent**, the Tax Reform Act of 2014 ensures that job creators of all sizes are finally given the opportunity to compete on a level playing field with their international competitors. This new, lower rate ends America's dubious distinction of having the highest corporate rate in the developed world.

Reducing the corporate rate is just one step toward making America a more attractive place to invest and hire. Coupled with the significant rate reduction, the Tax Reform Act of 2014 also gives certainty to our nation's largest employers of American workers by providing:

- An **improved, permanent R&D tax credit,** finally giving American manufacturers the certainty they need to compete against their foreign competition who have long had permanent R&D incentives, and

- **Repeal of the corporate AMT,** which raises taxes on American manufacturers during economic downturns, when they can least afford it.

These provisions are especially helpful for many large job creators who principally do business inside the United States, but for those companies competing internationally, these provisions are only one part of a plan that allows them to compete in the global marketplace.

Our plan also modernizes international tax rules to bring back nearly $2 trillion in "trapped cash" to invest and hire here in America:

- ☑ **lowering tax rates for American businesses to make them more competitive**

- ☑ **closing loopholes some companies use to ship jobs and profits overseas**

- ☑ **eliminating the double tax that only applies to the overseas earnings of U.S. companies if those companies want to reinvest those earnings in the United States, thus allowing them to bring home the nearly $2 trillion in "trapped cash" to invest and hire here in America**

The plan also takes steps to keep jobs here in the United States by including strong safeguards that shut down loopholes companies currently use to shift their profits to tax havens. It also removes incentives companies currently have to move their innovation offshore, by providing a neutral 15-percent tax rate on profits from innovation regardless of whether the manufacturing takes place in the United States or overseas.

Make the tax code more accountable to the taxpayer

We need a tax code that works for taxpayers, not the IRS. Our plan to fix the broken tax code includes reforms designed to make the IRS accountable to the taxpayer, to protect taxpayers' identities and to end agency mismanagement that led to the IRS political targeting scandal.

There is little that angers taxpayers more than Washington wasting their hard-earned dollars — especially when Washington does little or nothing to stop the mismanagement.

The Tax Reform Act of 2014 includes common sense provisions to prevent fraud, abuse and improper payments in numerous ways. For instance, it:

- Reforms the Earned Income Tax Credit (EITC) by making it a credit against actual payroll taxes paid, strengthening the program's integrity and better guarding against mismanagement.

- Requires a Social Security Number (SSN) to be provided when claiming the Additional Child Tax Credit (ACTC).

- Requires SSNs appearing on a taxpayer's W-2 to be truncated to show only the last four digits.

The plan also restores accountability to the IRS so that the agency can begin taking initial steps to restore the public's trust. In addition to the pain it caused each victim, at its core, the IRS political targeting scandal has revealed that the broken tax code created opportunities for IRS mischief at the expense of ordinary Americans. **The Tax Reform Act of 2014 takes strong steps to prevent the IRS from using its authority to abuse and intimidate taxpayers.** Our plan guarantees that if a taxpayer's rights are violated, the victim will have the ability to know what actions the IRS has taken to address his or her case. It also strengthens the accountability of the agency by requiring the Commissioner to ensure that IRS employees understand and act in accordance with those rights. The plan includes other much-needed reforms by providing for an ongoing review of the IRS's process for selecting taxpayers for audit, and helping to ensure this process is impartial —not undertaken at the whim of IRS employees or based on spurious allegations.

HOW WE GOT HERE

Developing our tax reform plan, which makes the code simpler and fairer and strengthens the economy, didn't happen overnight. After all, the American people are not interested in what Washington thinks works — only to find out that what works in Washington, DC, doesn't work in Washington state or Washington, Missouri. In order to secure the best input, tax writers in Congress went to great lengths to ensure that the real experts — individuals, families and job creators of all sizes and industries were a part of the conversation.

This transparent, "everyone gets a seat at the table" process involved **more than 30 separate Congressional hearings dedicated to tax reform, 11 separate bipartisan tax reform working groups, a nationwide tax tour** to hear directly from families and job creators about how to make the tax code work for them, and three **separate discussion drafts** looking at discrete areas of the tax code.

Bipartisan:

 30 Congressional Hearings

 11 Bipartisan Working Groups

 Nationwide Tour

 3 Discussion Drafts

 More than 14,000 comments at TaxReform.Gov

Overwhelmingly, the stakeholders made one point loud and clear – for the certainty of a lower rate, they were willing give up certain tax preferences that they have long held dear. This plan reflects the tradeoffs that were made in order to give families and job creators a simpler and fairer tax system that provides them with a lower rate and the certainty they need to plan, invest and hire.

Simplify Code and Lower Rates: A Wide Lens View

Many people are for tax reform as long as it doesn't change that one special provision they care about. If we left everything in the code exactly the same we would get the same broken tax code we have today. That is why tax reform requires a wide-lens view. Rather than focusing too closely on particular provisions, the Tax Reform Act of 2014 is structured to make sure that tax rates are lower and the code is simpler and fairer for all. Below is a step-by-step analysis of the tradeoffs in our plan. These tradeoffs result in a simpler, fairer tax code that lowers rates for every family and business in America, allowing 95 percent of taxpayers to do their taxes without having to fill out the complex "Schedule A." These tradeoffs result in **stronger economic growth that will add $3.4 trillion to the economy, create 1.8 million new private sector jobs and put $1,300 more a year in the pockets of middle-class families.**

Simplify Code and Lower Rates: Close Lobbyist Loopholes

Speaking about the impact of special interest provisions in the code, President Reagan described it well, saying:

> You see, the current code – taking up loads of shelf space and filled with paragraphs like the one I just read – is hardly a code at all. It's a hodge-podge of special favors, a product of the great Washington taffy-pull: the favor-seeking and influence peddling. So, it's unfair, yes. But even worse, all this special privilege makes the code the single biggest obstacle to economic growth in our nation today.

To lower tax rates, **our plan closes loopholes and cuts the size of the code by 25 percent,** making it simpler, fairer, and more effective and efficient. This includes a range of provisions, including some that have been advanced by Democrats and Republicans alike.

- Eliminating special depreciation benefits related to corporate jets.
- Requiring hedge fund managers and private equity firms to treat "carried interest" compensation as ordinary income, rather than as capital gain.
- Fixing the "John Edwards loophole," which allows wealthy individuals to establish partnerships or S corporations and mischaracterize payments from those entities as business profits, rather than compensation, thereby avoiding employment taxes on that income.

- Minimizing Wall Street's ability to hide and disguise potentially significant risks through the abuse of derivatives and other novel financial instruments by requiring that these financial products be taxed on a mark-to-market basis.

- Limiting corporate deductions for excessive stock options.

- Prohibiting tax deductions for costs incurred by illegal businesses.

- Preventing makers of violent video games from qualifying for the R&D tax credit.

- Requiring cruise ship companies — which generally pay no U.S. tax, despite extensive use of U.S. ports and all-too-frequent reliance on the U.S. Coast Guard for assistance — to pay tax on their U.S. income.

- Ending tax breaks that result in museum curators living in penthouses and university presidents living in mansions tax-free.

- Prohibiting employers from avoiding paying into Social Security and Medicare through the hiring of foreign seasonal student workers instead of American citizens.

- Repealing the special tax deduction for the purchase of prime seating tickets at college athletic events.

- Ending the tax code's "divorce subsidy" — which benefits divorce lawyers while helping to break up families — that allows divorcing couples to get a tax break for alimony payments.

Simplify Code and Lower Rates: Stop Subsidies for Excessive Compensation

Today, Wall Street tycoons and executives of leading non-profit entities and institutions receive compensation packages riddled with special tax-exempt treatment — courtesy of hardworking taxpayers. Rather than subsidize just a handful of select individuals, the Tax Reform Act of 2014 cleans up the tax code so more families and job creators benefit. The plan:

- Repeals the loophole that allows companies to deduct big stock bonuses when they cannot deduct cash bonuses.

- Imposes a 25 percent excise tax on compensation in excess of $1 million paid by a tax-exempt organization to one of the top five highest paid employees, to end the tax subsidy for million-dollar salaries at non-profit entities.

- Limits deferral of compensation through non-qualified deferred compensation plans often used by senior executives, by taxing all individuals when compensation is no longer subject to a substantial risk of forfeiture.

Simplify Code and Lower Rates: Bonds

Taxpayers across the country should not be forced to subsidize borrowing by state and local governments that provide a direct benefit to private individuals and entities. To reduce tax rates and create stronger economic growth, the tax reform bill:

- Repeals the interest exclusion for future issuances of "private activity bonds" (PABs) – bonds that directly benefit private individuals or entities.

Though changes are made to PABs as a tradeoff to lower rates, the Tax Reform Act of 2014:

- Maintains the current-law tax exemption for public purpose bonds issued by state and local governments (i.e., "muni bonds").

Simplify Code and Lower Rates: Business Credits

The Tax Reform Act of 2014 stops the practice of using the tax code to pick winners and losers based on political power rather than economic merit – such as alternative energy credits that hand out subsidies to wealthy investors in technologies that have never proven to be commercially viable – by repealing all business credits **_except_**:

- The R&D credit, which is made permanent to encourage innovation.

- The Low-income Housing Tax Credit, which is improved to help more low-income families at less cost to the taxpayer.

- The tax credit for improvements required by the Americans with Disabilities Act, which helps businesses absorb the cost of making improvements for those with special needs.

Simplify Code and Lower Rates: Carried Interest

Today, the tax code treats the profits earned by private equity investors as investment income, making it taxable at the capital gains rate, rather than treating those profits as ordinary income that is taxable at the higher individual tax rate. The plan:

- Re-characterizes as compensation (ordinary income) a portion of the gain of a partner that is actively engaged in the buying, developing and selling of other businesses.

- Assumes compensation in an amount equal to total capital invested in a fund multiplied by a rate of return.

- Does not apply to real estate development.

Simplify Code and Lower Rates: Depreciation

Depreciation rules affect nearly all American businesses and are intended to align the cost of business property and equipment as it declines in value due to wear and tear with the income that the property or equipment produces. However, the current rules are extremely complex and riddled with special provisions for particular types of property. Our plan:

- Simplifies these depreciation rules and eliminates special provisions to provide a fairer system for U.S. businesses, all while significantly reducing tax rates.

- Allows small businesses to expense (i.e., deduct immediately) up to $250,000 of new property and makes permanent the temporary rules that allow for expensing of improvements to real property and computer software.

- Modifies depreciation rules that businesses apply to recover the cost of new business property and equipment to better reflect the actual useful lives of such property by adopting depreciation schedules similar to those currently used under the AMT (which our plan repeals). In most cases, these schedules still provide for recovery of costs faster than the economic life of the asset.

In addition, to ensure that inflation does not eat away at the value of a business's capital investment, depreciation deductions are increased by the effect of inflation on depreciable property. Recognizing that any change in tax policy requires planning, the proposal only applies to property placed in service in 2017 and beyond, which will allow companies to prepare for and implement any necessary changes in a reasonable timeframe.

Simplify Code and Lower Rates: AMT and State and Local Tax Deduction

The plan:
- Permanently repeals the AMT for all taxpayers, simplifying the tax code for 4 to 6 million American families per year. These families will never again be forced to do their taxes twice — and deal with a second calculation that forces an average tax increase of $7,300 on them.

- The plan offsets this change, in part, by also repealing the deduction for state and local income, property and sales taxes. <u>This deduction redistributes wealth to big-government, high-tax states from small-government, low-tax states.</u>

Simplify Code and Lower Rates: Employment Taxes

Under current law, self-employed individuals are permitted to deduct one-half of their employment taxes as a means of putting them in an economically equivalent position to a business that can deduct the employment taxes paid for its employees. However, due to an error in the rules for calculating self-employment taxes, the current rules do not provide the intended economic parity. The plan will provide more uniform rules with respect to employment taxes paid by businesses by applying the rules evenly and consistently across businesses — regardless of what type of business entity the owners choose. Specifically, the plan:

- Modernizes tax treatment to reflect the relationship between labor and capital. For owners who materially participate in the operation of the business, 70 percent of their income from the business would be treated as self-employment income for Self-Employment Contribution Act (SECA) purposes and 30 percent would be treated as business profits exempt from SECA.

- Closes the loophole that provides a tax incentive to hire certain foreign workers instead of putting American workers first.

- Allows only those student workers earning less than $1,200 per quarter to be exempt from employment taxes.

Simplify Code and Lower Rates: Ending Special Tax Treatment for Alternative Energy

Today, the tax code picks "winners and losers" by providing numerous special tax breaks solely to the alternative energy industry. The Tax Reform Act of 2014 ends these crony-capitalist handouts, charting a commonsense path to American energy independence that also makes the code more efficient and effective. The plan:

- Repeals lobbyist loopholes like special credits, deductions and rules available **only** for alternative energy, while maintaining other general business provisions that are available across all industries.

- Makes permanent an improved version of the R&D tax credit that will help spur investment and innovation in all sectors.

Simplify Code and Lower Rates: Life Insurance

In an effort to ensure the code is fairer, more efficient, and effective for all, our plan includes a number of provisions designed to ensure that insurance companies have the same basic tax rules as other businesses. Recognizing certain differences in the nature of the insurance business, however, the plan also contains measures that ensure the safety net this industry provides remains intact. Seeking to achieve that much-needed balance, the Tax Reform Act of 2014 does not change the current law tax incentives for individuals who purchase life insurance products to provide financial protection for themselves and their families, including continuing the long-standing practice of exempting "inside build-up."

Simultaneously, and in an effort to lower the corporate rate from 35 percent to 25 percent, the plan aligns the tax treatment of the insurance industry with the rules that apply to other companies. These changes include:

- Repealing the special 10-year rule for adjustments related to the computation of life insurance companies' reserves and replacing it with the general 4-year rule used by all other businesses for making tax accounting method adjustments.

- Conforming net operating loss (NOL) rules to mirror the rules used by other industries by allowing insurance companies to carry NOLs back up to two tax years or carry them forward up to 20 tax years.

Simplify Code and Lower Rates: Modernizing Inventory Rules

Historically, the last-in, first-out (LIFO) inventory accounting method was designed to ensure that a business had enough essential inventories to continue business operations. However, with current just-in-time inventory methods, businesses are able to function without vast reserves of inventory, which renders LIFO outdated and less necessary. Reforming deductions, credits and tax rules like the LIFO method helps lower tax rates both for the small shops on Main Street and for our largest corporations competing around the globe. The plan addresses the unique challenges LIFO repeal presents by:

- Providing a generous transition rule for all businesses where the business could elect to begin paying tax on the deferred LIFO income over a four-year period beginning in 2019, with 10 percent due in 2019, 15 percent due in 2020, 25 percent due in 2021, and 50 percent due in 2022.

- Provides additional relief to small businesses by permitting the income of businesses with 100 or fewer owners a special, reduced tax rate of 7 percent.

Simplify Code and Lower Rates: Ending Bailouts for Wall Street Banks

Dodd-Frank, the legislation passed in response to the financial crisis, created a heightened regulatory regime for Systemically Important Financial Institutions ("SIFIs"). By declaring SIFIs to be "too big to fail," Dodd-Frank allows these big banks and financial institutions to pay lower borrowing costs, with the difference left to be made up by the American taxpayer.

While tax reform cannot undo Dodd-Frank, it can and should ensure that Wall Street reimburses the American taxpayer for a portion of the subsidy it receives. The Tax Reform Act of 2014 requires that SIFIs reimburse American taxpayers for a portion of this subsidy by:

- Imposing a new excise tax on certain SIFIs, as defined by Dodd-Frank.

- Requiring these institutions to pay a quarterly 0.035-percent tax on their worldwide consolidated assets in excess of $500 billion.

The rapid growth and abuse by Wall Street of certain financial products has contributed to the near collapse of our financial system, endangering investors saving for their children's education and their own retirement. The Tax Reform Act of 2014 equalizes tax treatment across the wide portfolio of financial products to increase transparency and reduce the "gaming" that has occurred in the past. The plan accomplishes this modernized uniformity and increased taxpayer protection by:

- Extending mark-to-market accounting treatment already used for a broad array of financial products to derivatives.

- Equalizing tax treatment of financial derivatives.

- Simplifying business hedging tax rules.

- Eliminating "phantom" tax resulting from debt restructurings.

- Harmonizing the tax treatment of bonds traded at a discount or premium on the secondary market.

- Increasing the accuracy of determining gains and losses on sales of securities, and preventing the harvesting of tax losses on securities.

Simplify Code and Lower Rates: Reforming Tax-Exempt Organizations

Tax-exempt organizations play a vital role in American society – providing needed assistance to millions of people every day. However, many operate and more closely resemble taxable businesses, not tax-exempt charitable organizations. For example, recent media stories have shed light on the fact that the NFL is organized as a non-profit despite taking in more than $9.5 billion per year and compensating its commissioner to the tune of $30 million in 2011.

The Tax Reform Act of 2014 makes a number of commonsense reforms that simplify several rules and ease compliance burdens for the charities. The plan:

- Simplifies the private foundation excise tax by consolidating the current two-rate structure into a single 1 percent flat rate.

- Reforms Unearned Business Income Tax (UBIT) rules by closing loopholes that allow organizations to avoid tax on commercial activities (e.g., AARP).

- Imposes a 25 percent excise tax on compensation in excess of $1 million paid by a tax-exempt organization to one of the top five highest paid employees.

- Requires private universities with large endowments to comply with the private foundation excise tax on investment income.

- Repeals tax exemption for professional sports leagues, such as the NFL.

When the Tax Reform Act of 1986 was finally complete, the headline in the *Washington Post* said it best, calling tax reform the **"impossible that became the inevitable."**

Today, we have the opportunity to again transform America – to make our economy stronger, to create more jobs and to increase the paychecks for families across the country. That is the kind of tax code the American people need – and deserve.

We cannot afford to wait. Now is the time for Congress and the White House to work together so that the impossible can once again become the inevitable.

The Tax Reform Act of 2014 makes the code simpler and fairer by:

- Providing a significantly more generous standard deduction so that 95 percent of taxpayers will no longer be forced to itemize their individual tax deductions.

- Reducing the size of the federal income tax code by 25 percent.

- Tackling fraud, abuse and mismanagement at the IRS to protect hard-earned taxpayer dollars.

It will make our economy stronger resulting in:

- $3.4 trillion in additional economic growth.

- 1.8 million new jobs.

- $1,300 per year more in the pockets of middle-class American families.

The results are clear:

✓ **More Growth.**

✓ **More Jobs.**

✓ **More money in the pockets of middle-class families.**

www.ingramcontent.com/pod-product-compliance
Lightning Source LLC
Chambersburg PA
CBHW081819170526

45167CB00008B/3458